BAPTISM OF
FIRE

DR. D. K. OLUKOYA

THE
BAPTISM
OF FIRE

DR. D. K. OLUKOYA

THE BAPTISM OF FIRE

© 2010 DR. D. K. OLUKOYA
ISBN 978-978-8424-14-7
August 2010

Published by:
The Battle Cry Christian Ministries
322, Herbert Macaulay Way, Yaba P. O. Box 12272, Ikeja, Lagos.
email: battlecrysales@mountainoffire.org
Phone: 2348033044239

All Scripture quotation is from the King James Version of the Bible

CONTENTS

CHAPTER ONE

THE FIRE
OF GOD

You must read this book carefully and prayerfully, especially if you are not satisfied with your present spiritual life and would want improvement.

Now Moses kept the flock of Jethro his father in law, the priest of Midian: and he led the flock to the backside of the desert, and came to the mountain of God, even to Horeb. And the angel of the Lord appeared unto him in a flame of fire out of the midst of a bush: and he looked, and, behold, the bush burned with fire, and the bush was not consumed. And Moses said, I will now turn aside, and see this sight, why the bush is not burnt. And when the Lord saw that he turned aside to see, God called unto him out of the midst of the bush and said, Moses, Moses. And he said, Here am I. And he said, Draw not nigh hither; put off thy shoes from off thy feet, for the place whereon thou standest is holy ground. Moreover he said, I am the God of thy father, the God of Abraham, the God of Isaac, and the God of Jacob. And Moses hid his face; for he was afraid to look upon God. Exodus 3: 1-6.

We find one of the most important events in the Scriptures, in the foregoing. The Bible is divided into what Bible students call, dispensations, which means, different periods of time. This particular time signaled the beginning of what we call, the Dispensation of the Law; it tells us about one man called Moses.

People have said a lot of things about the bush that was burning, but refused to be consumed, because in the desert, you find a lot of dry leaves, dry trees, cobwebs, bird nests and all kinds of things that are inflammable. These things were in

6

that bush, while the fire was on, yet they were not consumed; they were good materials for fire, yet the fire rejected the bush and its contents as its fuel supply.

THE ENERGY OF FIRE

The fuel that supplied energy for the fire was not in that bush, the fire sustained itself, and so, it was not an ordinary fire. The focus of the fire was on Moses, who saw it, turned aside and there he received his call. And the Bible tells us that of all the prophets, there was none like Moses who spoke to God face to face; he was a very important man of God. If you read his history, you will find out that even the devil tried to kill him at a young age, just as the devil tried to kill Jesus at a young age.

Sometimes, when we say, "Pray against the spirit of Herod," many people don't understand what we mean. The spirit of Herod is the spirit that kills good things at infancy. Herod was the man who killed all babies below two years old, because he wanted to kill Jesus. The devil tried to kill Moses at the side of the water, where they put him, but God prevented it. The devil tries to kill many people, because he knows what God will do with their lives.

Moses went to the best university in the world, because Egypt was the best centre of knowledge in the world at that time. He lived in the palace of the king and was learned in all the wisdom of the Egyptians.

THE WILDERNESS

The burning bush incident, that we are describing, happened at Mount Horeb. Horeb means a waste or a wilderness. All men of God must pass through the wilderness; Moses passed through his own wilderness, Elijah, John the Baptist and even Jesus our Lord, passed through their own wilderness. Jesus was there for 40 days and 40 nights. All holy men of God and anybody who wants to be useful to God must get to that place in his life, the place where fire is burning the bush and the bush is not consumed.

Moses died at the age of 120 years; He spent his first 40 years in Egypt, which ended in disaster because he ended up as a murderer. Why? Because he tried to use his own power, he tried to use the arm of flesh, which we know always fails. He ended up as a murderer. He ran away from Egypt at the age of 40, to a place called Midian and there, he did the kind of job that Egyptians hate so much; the dirty job of a shepherd, which a graduate would not like to do. He did not know that God was teaching him the principles of shepherding, for a time was coming when he would lead three million people in the wilderness, just like Peter was first taught how to catch fish and from there, learnt how to catch men

THE BURNING BUSH

Moses saw the burning bush when he was 80. That was the moment he met God and his life was never the same again; His life became meaningful and from there, had a purpose, He knew why he was called. He discovered the purpose of God for his life. There are many people who do not know God's purpose for their lives and as such, are doing the wrong things. In summary, Moses spent the first 40 years of his life thinking that he was somebody; he spent the second 40 years learning that he was nobody; then he spent the last 40 years, seeing what God could do with a Mr. Nobody like him. He did not know what to do until he came across that fire.

All darkness shall be hid in his secret places: a fire not blown shall consume him; it shall go ill with him that is left in his tabernacle. Job 20:26.

Job discovered the fire that nobody prepared with fuel. It is men who have moved like this that can be useful to God in any form.

John answered, saying unto them all, I indeed baptize you with water but one mightier than I cometh, the latchet of whose shoes I am not worthy to unloose, he shall baptize you with the Holy Ghost and with fire. Whose fan is in his hand, and he will thoroughly purge his floor, and will gather the wheat into his garner, but the chaff he will burn with fire unquenchable. Luke 3:16-17

John the Baptist was a powerful messenger. The Bible tells us that he wore clothes that were woven from camel's hair, and leather belt; his food was locust and honey. Jesus told us that amongst those born of women; none was greater than John the Baptist. He was the forerunner of our Lord Jesus Christ.

HOW TO BE QUALIFIED

A study of the life of John the Baptist reveals that, he had a lot of wonderful qualities; an unforgettable one was that, he was very precise in everything he did. He said, "I baptise you, but my own baptism is with water. Somebody else is coming who will baptise you with the Holy Ghost and with fire." A lot of people know about water baptism. We thank God for it, because when we are baptized in water, it is the symbol that we have died with Christ and resurrected with Him. It is good. Also, when you are baptised with the Holy Spirit, you may speak in tongues, you may prophesy and all kinds of things may happen, but very few people know what we mean by baptism of fire.

In fact, many who claim to know what it means do not really know. But verse 17 makes it very clear; chaff is the refuse of grain and the straw of the corn. In those days, in the land of Israel, when people wanted to remove the chaff from the corn, they would thread upon the corn until the chaff was removed. Then they would separate the chaff from the grain and burn it with fire, because if they did not burn it with fire, the wind would blow it into the grain which they had cleaned.

THE WHEAT

The wheat represents the good in our lives, that which is produced by the Holy Spirit. The chaff represents the evil in us, produced by the flesh. The Lord knows how to separate the wheat from the chaff; sometimes when He does it to us, we feel the heat in one particular area of our lives, which we love dearly and are not ready to let go. We all have some items in the showroom of our lives that are not valuable to God. Sometimes when God begins to touch these things, we complain that the pain is too much, whereas it is the refining heat of God.

When God passes you through fire, you will come out a better vessel, to serve the water of life to people. God will use both cold and hot vessels. If you are in the house of God now and you are hot for the Lord, He will use you and if you are cold, He will use you. You may wonder how He will use you if you are cold; He will use you as an example for others not to follow.

He did this to the children of Israel many times, when they did the wrong thing; He disciplined them so that nobody would follow them. But if you are hot, He will use you to minister grace to others and as an example for others to follow. The only kind of people, God will not use at all, are the lukewarm people. He will abandon them on the shelf, they will be stock on the shelf like expired wares. So you should allow the fire of God to do a deep work within you today.

THE DARK DAYS

A long time ago, Nigeria was in heavy darkness. Human sacrifice was common and a lot of horrible things happened; anyone who wore a good dress today would not wake up the next morning. People were afraid to call witches by name; they called them nicknames, because they were afraid that they would die. In some places in Nigeria, witches actually went about in daytime, people grounded day old babies in mortar to use for medicine, some people received up to 2,000 incisions and there were many evil trees growing around. Sometimes when men of God cut these trees, blood would come out from them, or sometimes the following morning, they would start growing again as if they had not been cut. People's lives were regulated by superstition; you could not whistle at night or call a snake by its name. Some hunters shot at animals which turned into human beings. Many rocks and stones demanded worship and if they were not worshipped, there was trouble.

We were told about a king who had a special cutlass, which used to spark fire, and people were afraid of him. But then, something happened; God raised up certain men in this country who received more than the Holy Spirit; the gifts of speaking in tongues and body vibrations. They received the baptism of fire. These men entered forbidden forests, stopped the killing of twins, silenced powerful demons and chased them out of their hiding places. One of these men got to this king and commanded the cutlass to be powerless; its sparkling ceased immediately.

PRAYER POINTS

You spirits of laziness in prayer, get out of my life, in the name of Jesus.

I. Every satanic deposit blocking my communication line with heaven, melt away by the fire of Holy Ghost, in the name of Jesus.

II. Every addiction to physical things that are causing lukewarmness to prayer, die, in the name of Jesus.

III. Father, help me to always have meaningful time in Your presence, in the name of Jesus.

IV. Every embargo, placed on my spiritual life, be lifted away by fire, in the name of Jesus.

V. I release myself from the bondage of food and sleep, in the name of Jesus.

VI. My spiritual life will not collapse, in the name of Jesus.

VII. Lord, give a thirst and hunger for prayer, in the name of Jesus.

VIII. I rededicate my life to God the Father, God the Son and God the Holy Spirit, in the name of Jesus.

IX. Every spirit of impatience in the presence of God, die, in the name of Jesus.

X. Father, always give me alertness in my spirit when I'm in Your presence, in the name of Jesus.
Every spirit of prayer-procrastination, I bind you, in the name of Jesus.

CHAPTER TWO
THE REAL BAPTISM

The blunt truth is that, there are many people with the baptism of the Holy Spirit, but very few people who have received the baptism of fire. Those who have received the baptism of fire would not mind, whether someone is annoying them or not, there are some characters that you will notice in them.

Virtually anywhere in the Old Testament that God appeared, fire was always present. Fire symbolizes the presence of God, the Unquenchable Fire. We remember the God of Elijah, the one that answered by fire.

A piece of iron will not bend easily, unless you push it into the fire and it becomes hot; the reason some people have not been bent is because there is no fire in them. Therefore, God says, "Okay, I abandon you to your situation." God will not abandon me to my situation, in Jesus' name.

When you go through the baptism of fire, God will reschedule your life. A lot of people are rescheduling their lives, after their parents who made mistakes and are now in hell fire. They will say, "Because my daddy was a member of this place, I must be there and die there." May God have mercy on them. God is crying, "Be rescheduled, be rescheduled," but they refuse to be rescheduled.

People hate change so much, but that is what brings progress. It's because they have not passed through the baptism of fire and so God finds it difficult to bend them, He just abandons them. The lame will be beating the drum, while the leper sings and a child of God, who has not been rescheduled, will be dancing. This is very unfortunate, but there are many of such people around now. Until you listen and become rescheduled, many things won't find their way out; this is the blunt truth of the word of God. Raw gold just dug out of the earth never looks good, but when it is passed through fire to remove the impurities, it comes out clean. The reason unclean spirits and

14

all kinds of things are still hiding in some people's lives, is that, there is no fire in them. Beloved, we need the fire of God in our midst and when it comes in, the promise of the word of God will come to pass; the strangers will fade away and run out of their hiding places. When the fire comes in, it does not spare the ant, the elephant or the snake; it burns everything. But many people are afraid of what will happen if they get on fire; if you are like that, you need to be rescheduled. This may be your final call.

Fire will produce heat and make people hot. The reason some people are so slow, when it comes to spiritual development and the things of God is that there is no fire, no baptism of fire. All they do is, speaking in tongues: "Baba bakakaka," and immediately after that, they sleep and the night caterers come and say, "Well, you have blown your tongue; it is time for your night meal." And the person, who was speaking in tongues, begins to consume food, which weakens his spiritual life.

How can unbelievers be running after a Christian girl? You are praying for a Christian husband but, it is only married men and unbelievers who find you beautiful. Something is wrong somewhere, something has to be burnt in your life, to remove that magnet inviting evil people to you.

FIRE COOKS

The reason some people make a big start and have poor finishing is that there is no fire. Fire symbolizes power and lack of it means powerlessness. Fire produces light and without it, there would be darkness.
Have you received the baptism of fire? Lack of this baptism is why many Christians are suffering. A Christian, who is not interested in progress, has no fire. A Christian, who is not

15

excited about the things of God, has no fire. A Christian, who gets weighed down by long prayer, has no fire. If certain things are still coming upon you and pressing you down on your bed, it is because there is no fire. Witches and wizards roam around the house freely, when they know that the person is cold. Some people will be in a hurry to escape from God's presence; when they are in the house of God, they are always in a hurry to go. To some, prayer and fasting becomes very difficult because there is no fire. Some come to MFM and say, "I thank God that my prayer life has changed." We are not asking for your prayer life to only improve, but for it to be on fire.

Perhaps your Holy Ghost baptism is just speaking in tongues; you forget that there is a difference between, possessing the Holy Spirit and the Holy Spirit possessing you. The Holy Spirit will not possess you, until you have passed through the baptism of fire, because when the chaff is still there, it means that fire has not consumed it. That way, the Holy Spirit cannot possess you fully; it can only enter and operate in a little way, but for total possession, fire has to come.

You want to reign with Christ always, but never in your life have you seen a vision of heaven; what you see are masquerades, night caterers and serpents. With which Jesus do you want to reign? When others say, "I saw angels of the living God, praising God in heaven and I joined them; it was so wonderful," you are saying, "I saw snakes." You should be ashamed of preaching the gospel.

Many are just conquerors, but not more than conquerors. Someone who is more than a conqueror, will not only conquer, he will also take captives. How many captives have you won for the Lord? You are still busy sewing tight skirts so that everybody can see your shape. How many captives have you won for the Lord? Many people are praying that, they want to grow, but it is not coming from their hearts, something within them is saying, "No, you cannot grow." It is lack of the baptism of fire that makes it difficult for people, to run away from strange things and situations. The virtues of many men, have been buried under the sea by strange powers that have collected their sperm and have stored it there, while they are busy going about. It is because there is no fire in their lives.

When you receive the baptism of fire, three things will happen:

1.   **There will be no spiritual lethargy.**

> *Then I said I will not make mention nor speak any more in his name. But his word was in mine heart as a burning fire shut up in my bones, and I was weary with forbearing, and I could not stay.* **Jeremiah 20: 9.**

When you receive the baptism of fire you cannot relax, it is not possible because the fire will not let you. You cannot see sinners and feel unconcerned. You would not be able to do without prayer and you would find it difficult to be away from your Bible, you will want to sit down and read it through. That is what we call, baptism of fire.

2. **You will preach with fire in your bones.**

> *For though I preach the gospel I have nothing to glory of: for necessity is laid upon me, yea, woe is unto me, if I preach not the gospel.* **I Corinthians 9: 16.**

You cannot stop preaching. When the occult or witchcraft people see you, they will mark you and avoid you.

17

3. **There will be a spiritual overflow.**

Behold, my belly is as wine which hath no vent; it is ready to burst like new bottles. I will speak, that I may be refreshed: I will open my lips and answer.
Job 32: 19-20.

The power of God would be burning within you; you will wake up in the night speaking in tongues. God will be talking to you and you'll see what God wants you to do. You will not live in darkness or semi-darkness.

Have you received the baptism of fire? A pregnant woman who had the baptism of fire went to the market. There, she mistakenly stepped on what an idol worshipper displayed for sale, the idol worshipper jumped up and started to rain curses on her, while she was saying that she was sorry. He cracked his sticks and fire began to come out of his mouth. This pregnant woman said, "I quench that fire in your mouth, in the name of Jesus," and the fire quenched. The man said, "What did you do now?" The woman said, "I spoke to your fire, in Jesus' name, and secondly, I return all your curses back to you, in Jesus' name." When the man heard that, he ran away. If the woman had no baptism of fire, it would have been a terrible day for her. In fact, the power of darkness could have changed her baby from there.

PRAYER POINTS

1. Fire from God fall upon my life now, in the name of Jesus.
2. (*Stretch forth you hands as you say this:*). Lord, put the head of my Goliath in my hands, in the name of Jesus.
3. My enemy shall bow down before me, in the name of Jesus.
4. O God, make me a vessel of your power, in the name of Jesus.

CHAPTER THREE

DEALING WITH FIRE EXTINGUISHERS

Unfortunately, a lot of people are becoming friends of fire extinguishers. What quenches the fire of God?

FIRE EXTINGUISHERS

1. **Lust:** This is when your imagination indulges uncleanness.

2. **Idolatry:** If you permit anything to come between you and your God, it becomes an idol. For example, your job, money, etc.

3. **Laziness:** Life of ease at home, lack of zeal for the things of God and hatred for long prayer sessions.

4. **Over-sensitivity:** Bitterness rises quickly in the hearts of some people, immediately someone disagrees with them.

5. **Judgmental spirit.**

6. **Gossip:** All gossips are the devil's advertisers.

7. **Worry:** This is when you are too anxious about the future.

8. **Selfishness:** When you ignore the interest of others and you are interested only in yourself.

9. **Distraction:** This is when you are unable to focus on Christ and you find it difficult to read the Bible and gain something from it.

10. **Lying.**

11. **Discouragement:** Some people are easily discouraged; at the first sign of failure, they run away. They quit immediately things are hard.

12. **Abusive tongue:** Some people cannot control their temper.

13. **Depression:** This is when you allow despair to overtake you. You think of your problems always and withdraw from everybody, when the Bible says, "I will not despair for I have believed to see the goodness of the Lord in the land of the living."

14. **Fear:** All kinds of fear are in people's lives.

15. **Procrastination:** This is when you are always planning to go higher and dig deeper, but you always end up postponing the day you will start.

16. **Lack of sexual control:** People in this category should forget about spiritual growth.

The enemies of our soul have the most powerful scanning machine, which you can ever think of; they can look and locate our weaknesses quickly. They struggle so much, so that people will not receive the baptism of fire. When the baptism of fire falls on a person, he can prophesy for five hours non-stop; many things will be drawn out of his life. He would not have to pray to be delivered, the fire will answer everything. All infirmities would disappear; when fire falls on fibroid or whatever it may be, it will melt away, because God did not create it with you. It is chaff and fire has to burn it.

Beloved, if you are ready today, I want you to bow down your head and begin to ask the Lord to forgive you of any sin that will prevent the fire from falling upon you. Because while praying the prayers, the fire will fall and things will burn, you will be catapulted to a higher realm. You will go from the position of weakness, to that of power.

When some people came against Elijah and extended the invitation of failure to him, he said, "Instead of me to come down, let fire come down." And that was how 102 people were roasted on the ground. The third group of 51 people that came to him adopted a different approach, because they were afraid to die. When you are in Elijah's position, who is the enemy that can sit on your brain or your business? There will be no need for you to go to the hospital, when you have the great Physician.

Please, if you are not ready for the fire that will come down as you pray, don't pray.

PRAYER POINTS

1. Holy Ghost fire, fall upon me, in the name of Jesus.
2. All strangers lose your hold, in the name of Jesus.
3. O Lord, crucify me on your altar now, in the name of Jesus.
4. O Lord, set me on fire by the Holy Ghost, in the name of Jesus.
5. Everything that is cooperating with evil in my life, s t o p your cooperation, in the name of Jesus.
6. My life, begin to cooperate with the Holy Ghost, in the name of Jesus.
7. All the negative things that I have been eating, I refuse to eat you anymore, in Jesus' name.

CHAPTER FOUR

MOVING HIGHER

God has a plan for you; it is to make you go from strength to strength. God wants you to move from one level of fire to another.

They go from strength to strength, every one of them in Zion appeareth before God. **Psalm 84:7.**

SALIENT POINTS

Let these words be registered in your mind:
1. If you want to survive in this present, wicked world, you need to move to the higher ground of power. If you must survive in your life, family and calling, you ought to possess a greater level of power and anointing.
2. There is a satanic revival of strange powers. Many are acquiring strange powers, in order to satisfy their personal and selfish ends; the works of these wicked entities are unimaginable.

Sometime ago, one of the political giants in Nigeria came for prayers, in order to occupy a political position in the country. I asked him what he was looking for in a church like ours; He said he wanted to do all he could to get the position. Men had told him to run a new car into the sea; He did that but to no avail. Recently, he was told another thing, to bring the head of an albino. This he refused, saying that he would not because of political office; cut the head of a human being. Hence, he decided to try prayers.

This is the extent to which people go, in order to get their lusts satisfied. It is not surprising that the Bible says,

24

Finally, my brethren, be strong in the Lord, and in the power of his might. **Ephesians 6:10.**

The Scriptures admonish us to be strong in the Lord. It does not admonish us to be strong in malice, fighting, fornication or lying, but to be strong in the Lord and in the power of His might.

When considering the power of God; human shapes and sizes, academic attainments and positions occupied in the society, are irrelevant. Oratory, loudness or pitch of human voice does not matter.

A CHAMPION

The power of God is resident in the inner man of believers. What really matters to God is what is resident in the inner man. The devil is much interested in the power content of your inner man, that's why people with satanic eyes can look at a believer and assess his strength. They can steal and use the power deposited in a believer's life.
Brethren should not pretend to be champions, when in fact they are weaklings; the devil is always around to test the spiritual ability of believers. When he does this, it would be shown whether they are truly champions or weaklings.

If as a believer, you've never quoted the Scriptures against spiritual attacks; your inner man is weak. Many people complain that they hate spirit husbands and wives, but cannot do anything against them. Quoting the Scriptures against these spirits, when you are weak internally will not yield any result.

THE POWER CONTENT

After demonstrating spiritual weakness against these spirits in the dream, several people wake up feeling worried and angry. Then they start praying, but how beautiful it would have been, if they were strong. The truth is that the power content of many people is low. Have you ever found yourself being pursued in the dream, in such a way that you were sweating by the time you woke up? If so, you are spiritually weak.

A sister learnt a great lesson many years ago. She woke up one morning and found a short creature by her bedside. This short creature called all the five names the sister was bearing, including those many people did not know her by. The creature said, "Stand up." She woke up, carefully looked at the creature and saw that it was holding a big club in its hand. She said, "In the name of Jesus, I command you to start to knock your head with the club in your hand, while I go to fetch my Bible." The creature started to beat itself, according to the instruction which the sister gave. If the power content of the sister was low, the next day, people would have come to mourn her saying, "Unfortunately, this sister has passed on to glory." And the believers would then gather together, to sing heavenly songs for her as she has departed. Such songs as, "We shall gather at the river," "When we all get to heaven what a day of rejoicing shall it be?" etc. They would not have known that, the power content of the sister was low and that was why the devil killed her.

Your power content determines how far you can go. When your power level is low, you are a spiritual dwarf; you will not be able to resist the enemy. You cannot resist the weakness the devil brings on you.

REAL OR FAKE

There are two kinds of pastors in the House of God. There are professional pastors and career pastors; there are text books pastors and there are those that are "called." These kinds of pastors can easily be differentiated; those who are pastors for their daily sustenance are different from those, who are pastors because they are called to be pastors.

There was a big, embarrassing tree at the back of a church, nobody ever thought of cutting it down. Sometimes, when the service was going on, idol worshippers would gather under the tree to sacrifice to their gods. The new pastor, posted to that church grew annoyed and ordered the cutting down of the tree. However, it was surprising that a loud scream was heard and a blood-like fluid was coming out of the tree, as it was being cut. Frustrated, the pastor left the tree and went back to the church, but the tree grew again before the service was over, that same day. And by the second day the pastor was dead.

The second pastor was posted to take over the church and having heard what killed his predecessor, he refused to have anything to do with the tree. When the third pastor came, he started to speak destruction to the evil tree, from the first day he got to the church. One day, he cut the tree down and as the usual blood was coming out of the tree, he confronted it with the anointing oil and there was a loud scream. The chief priest died that same day and through this, the work of God expanded in that locality.

THE YARDSTICK

The spiritual content of your inner man is very, very important. It is that power within you that determines your spiritual success; if there is a low power content in your inner man, you will be very weak at the altar of prayer. If I ask everybody in the church to pray continuously for 12 hours, some people will go away, some will grumble and say; "These people want to kill someone here with prayers," while very few will carry on till the end. Why the different response? The inner spiritual strength of the people varies.

When your power content is low, your prayer power will be low; you will not be happy when you're told to go to prayer meetings or when a long prayer session is going on. Many years ago, I was in a church where I was one of the choir members. We had a particular choir master, who was fond of saying, "Let somebody lead us in prayer, and the person must ensure that the prayer is very, very short." We were praying short prayers, but one day we started to fight ourselves; the "short prayers" led some people to throw books at others. There was confusion and pandemonium; that was where our short prayers took us.

PRAYER POINTS

Let my system be programmed for prayers, in the name of Jesus.

I. Let fire from the throne of God fall upon my prayer altar, in the name of Jesus.

II. Every enemy of my prayer life, die, in the name of Jesus.

III. I refuse to be the enemy of my prayers, in the name of Jesus.

IV. O God that answers by fire, deliver me from the power of prayerlessness, in the name of Jesus.

V. Every satanic cage, caging my prayer life, catch fire, in the name of Jesus.

VI. Holy Spirit, help my infirmities to pray and prevail in prayers, in the name of Jesus.

VII. O Lord, kindle in my life, the fire of prayer that will never go out, in the name of Jesus.

VIII. Lord, make me a prayer eagle, in the name of Jesus.

IX. Wandering mind during prayers, I bind you out of my life, in the name of Jesus.

X. O Lord, wake up my prayer life, in the name of Jesus.

XI. Every usuriousness in prayer, die, in the name of Jesus.

XII. Every fainting spirit in my morning devotion, die, in the name of Jesus.

XIII. I shall not be discouraged in the place of prayer, in the name of Jesus.

XIV. Power that prays to get results, fall upon my life now, in the name of Jesus.

XV.   O Lord, turn my minimum to maximum in prayer, in the name of Jesus.

XVI.   Every seed of prayerlessness in my life, die by fire, in the name of Jesus.

XVII. Every arrow of lukewarmness fired into my prayer life, die, in the name of Jesus.

You spirit of extreme drowsiness, loose your hold upon my life, in the name of Jesus.

CHAPTER FIVE

THE SUBTLE FIRE QUENCHERS

The devil has introduced a new fire quencher; this fire quencher has put out the fire of several fire brands. Discouragement is a subtle weapon of quenching the fire of God's children. How does the enemy get this done? You will soon discover his strategy.

And it came to pass, when David and his men were come to Ziklag on the third day, that the Amalekites had invaded the south, and Ziklag, and smitten Ziklag, and burned it with fire. And had taken the women captives, that were therein: they slew not any, either great or small, but carried them away, and went on their way. So David and his men came to the city, and, behold, it was burned with fire; and their wives, and their sons, and their daughters, were taken captives. Then David and the people that were with him lifted up their voice and wept, until they had no more power to weep. And David's two wives were taken captives, Ahinoam the Jezreelitess, and Abigail the wife of Nabal the Carmelite. And David was greatly distressed; for the people spake of stoning him, because the soul of all the people was grieved, every man for his sons and for his daughters: but David encouraged himself in the LORD his God. And David said to Abiathar the priest, Ahimelech's son, I pray thee, bring me hither the ephod. And Abiathar brought thither the ephod to David. And David inquired at the LORD, saying, Shall I pursue after this troop? shall I overtake them? And he answered him, Pursue: for thou shalt surely overtake them, and without fail recover all. 1 Samuel 30: 1-8.

Verse 18 says that David recovered all that the Amalekites had carried away.

Discouragement is a terrible disease and a very powerful weapon in the hand of the enemy of our soul. Consider this illustration; something went bad for a lady and she became so sad and cried herself to sleep. As she slept, she saw a vision where she was in a big market and as she moved round the market, she found a shop called, Mr. Devil's Shop. She said, "Wonderful, the devil has a shop in this place." She went in to see what the devil was selling and found on the shelf; Anger, Hypertension and Diabetes with their prices attached. She said, "Mr. Devil, what is the most expensive material in your shop?" He brought something out, on which was written "Discouragement," and said: "This is the most expensive thing, when I get Christians discouraged and worried, I send fear into them and from there, all kinds of other things will go in to them."

It is sad but true that, many people actually wage war against themselves. Imagine that you take your car to a mechanic and he says, "I should have been a bricklayer, all the cars I repair, pack up; in fact, I don't know what I am doing here." What will you do? Of course, you will take your car away. Or you go to the hospital for surgery and the surgeon complains: "I should have been a motor mechanic. All the patients I operate on die." I am sure that you will go somewhere else. Many people downgrade themselves continually with their mouths. Whenever the devil wants to box you to a corner, encourage yourself in the Lord.

WHAT IS THE MEANING OF THE WORD "DISCOURAGE?"

It is a simple English word that is made up of "dis" meaning lack, and "courage." It therefore means lack of courage. The trouble with discouraged people is that, they cannot hear from God. The Bible says, "Therefore with joy shall you draw water from the well of salvation." The devil knows that discouraged people cannot commune with God properly, or hear His voice. Encouragement brings hope, but discouragement causes hopelessness and despair. It is so easy to know the size of a person's faith, by observing how much trouble it takes to discourage him.

I read an article about a man, who tried to sell soap to a certain customer. He started by going to the customer in the morning and continued until the customer got tired and said, "Ah! This is the 10th soap seller that has come here. What is the problem? Okay, how much is the soap? I will buy, so that they will stop worrying me." So he bought the soap. The man then said: "Point of correction sir, I am the only one that has been coming. In the morning, I wore a suit and you turned me away. I went and changed and came back, I have been here 10 times. Thank you for buying." This is the kind of people who can make headway.

When people are encouraged, they stand on their feet and smile, even when it looks like they are faced with defeat; but discouraged people have a lot of loose ends to tie up. When discouraged people are sick, they give up and die quickly. I have seen where some people, were trying to purge a lady, who swallowed a large number of drug tablets, because she wanted to die. As they were doing that, she kept saying,

"Leave me, let me die, let me die." Why? She was discouraged. Discouraged people sometimes forget that, certain mistakes might have been made in the past and God would require time to correct them. So, they conclude that God has gone on holiday. Discouraged people believe that life is a failure. To be quite honest with you, I think discouragement has killed more people than typhoid and malaria.

Discouraged people snatch defeat from certain victory, they see victory coming and snatch defeat out of it.
They borrow problem from the future, they are worried about tomorrow, even though they have no idea of what will happen tomorrow. They borrow the problems of the future and transfer them to the present; this does not make sense at all, it is too early to start worrying about tomorrow.

Discouraged people drink the wine of frustration. When you hear someone always saying, "I don't like this, I don't want this at all," there is frustration in place. It is very easy to know frustrated ladies; they paint their hair in different colors, use wigs, scrap their eyebrows, put lead pencil, paint their lips and nails, etc. They also wear tight or transparent dresses that expose their bodies.

THE DISGRACE

Discouraged people advertise the devil's disgrace; the devil is already disgraced and they are advertising it. They have faith, but the faith is in failure. Before David could hear God, he had to encourage himself, he shook off discouragement and believed that God would turn his calamity into goodness. Therefore, it is only a heart that is encouraged that is conditioned to hear good news.

In Exodus 6:9, we see the situation of the children of Israel in Egypt. God had already raised a deliverer for them. But what happened when the deliverer came?

> *And Moses spake so unto the children of Israel:*
> *but they hearkened not unto Moses for anguish*
> *of spirit, and for cruel bondage.* **Exodus 6:9.**

They could not accept the good news, because their spirits were down. But when David encouraged himself in the Lord, he prayed with confidence and the wonderful promise came from the Lord: "You shall surely pursue, and overtake and by all means recover." David would not have heard anything if he had chosen to be discouraged.

FACTS ABOUT DISCOURAGEMENT

A person can decide to give up on something that would help him or her. When a woman says: "I am tired of begging this man. Every day I kneel down and say forgive me, forgive me; even when I have not committed any offence, I still say forgive me, forgive me. Why am I always the one begging? I am tired of begging." It is better for such a woman to keep begging. If she gives up, discouragement will set in. One man said: "I am tired of greeting people without any response from them; after all, I am not wood. I am tired. I greet them and they answer with their heads and eyes, don't they have mouth to answer?" Please, keep greeting them.

Some people will say, "Prayer has finished in the house of prayer warriors, deliverance has finished with deliverance ministers." Keep praying. Or someone may say, "I am tired of coming to meetings and laying hands on the same place every day." Keep laying hands, your breakthrough may come with the next laying of hands. The mountains that we are facing get weaker, as we pray against them. So, it is dangerous to be discouraged, because the period you allow discouragement to set in, could be the time when you are about to get your breakthrough. I would like you to take note of some important truths about discouragement:

1. **Discouragement is very expensive in the devil's market because you pay with your life.**

   Someone may say, "I have been paying my tithes. I have been very faithful in doing so, but I have not had any big breakthrough." What you should do, is to give more violently. But if you say you will no longer give, you will be like the man whom God blessed and by the time he made his first breakthrough, the tithe was ₦5000. As he held the ₦5000, his hands were shaking and he said; "Ah, should I put the whole of this down? Ah! Do we really have to pay tithe?" He ran to the man of God and said, "Excuse me, sir; this money is too large to pay just like that. For example, I can invest it in this, that, that, that. Why can't I just pay part of it and thank God?" The man of God answered, "Do you want the Lord to return you to your former state, when you were earning ₦10, 000 per month and paying ₦1000 tithe?" He said, "No, that too is not good."

   If you have been sowing your seed and it is like no blessing is coming, sow more violently instead of being discouraged. See all impossible situations as opportunities in disguise.

2. **Discouragement is a personal decision.** You need to make a conscious decision not to be discouraged. This is why sometimes; they call people who have faith, mad people. They call them mad people because, when they are supposed to be rolling on the floor and crying, they are busy jumping and rejoicing. No one can discourage you, unless you decide to discourage yourself. Do not say, "Ah! It is our pastor. He does not give me much to do. He does not recognize me." If you go to a bus-stop, lay your hands on two mad people and they get healed, or you convert 200 people per week, no matter who your pastor is; he will recognize you. So, make a conscious effort not to be discouraged, take a decision this moment, to always encourage yourself in the Lord, then you can hear Him clearly.

3. **Do not wait for someone to come and encourage you.** There is scarcity of people who encourage others. Rather when you tell them your problem, for an example; your husband ran away, they would tell you that your own problem is even better. One will tell you, "My own husband is running after me with an axe." So, what kind of encouragement is that?

4. **Encourage yourself in the Lord and render thanksgiving to Him.** Tell Him you appreciate His blessings and faithfulness. Decide that circumstances will not enslave your soul, no matter what.

The Lord once said to me that many people who come to church need deliverance from grasshopper spirit.

WHAT IS GRASSHOPPER SPIRIT?

It is the spirit of "we are not able," the spirit that afflicted the Israelites, whom God told to go and take possession of the Promised Land. They said, "No, we are not able, we are like grasshoppers." You also need to stand against the spirit of evil expectation. It will be very sad, if something happens and a believer opens his mouth and says, "I knew that problem would come and now it has occurred." It is a very powerful spirit, which we must stand against. It is the devil, who should be wondering when we will shoot our next arrow, not us, saying that we don't know when to attack.

WHAT THEN IS THE CURE OF DISCOURAGEMENT?

There is no one that a trial and frustration period, will not face at one time, or the other. Somebody has said that life is a jungle; that is true.

1. **Release your situation into the hands of the Lord:** A songwriter says, "Take your burden to the Lord and leave it there." Refuse to doubt; refuse to waste your night, working it out with your brain. The Bible says, "Casting all your cares upon Him, for He cares for you." It does not say cast some, but all; if you do not hand your cares over to Him, then don't blame Him if He does not work on them.

2. **See divine possibilities:** See that the blessings you need can come. You must see that every problem has an end and that the end of a trial will come. Begin to see that, God can do something in your life that will make

the pain, the fear and the financial problems, come to an end. Begin to see that possibilities and positive things will begin to happen.

In the Bible, those who violently claimed their blessings did so, because they saw that it was possible. They pursued it seriously, they did not give up; they kept going and going, until what they wanted came into their hands. Look at the woman with the issue of blood. Before she left her home she had it settled: "I know that all I need do is to touch the helm of His garment and I shall be made whole. I don't even want the man to pray for me, it is not necessary." She had already seen the possibility.

It does not matter what any doctor, has said about your problem; It does not matter what any prophet has said. Neither the prophet, nor the doctor has the last say, about anybody's life; God has the last say. The woman saw the possibility and that was it. Jacob saw the possibility and stood firm until he got it. Blind Bartimaeus saw the possibility. The Syrophenician woman asked Jesus to heal her daughter and Jesus said, "No, I cannot take the food of the children and give it to dogs." The woman was not discouraged, she was not upset; she was determined to get what she wanted. She stayed there until the Saviour had to answer her prayer.

May be men of God, have disappointed you, frustrated you and made you bitter. There are some people, who have resolved never to step into the church again, because of what one pastor or the other did to them. If you are like that, encourage yourself in the Lord.

A man and his wife had a terrible fight one day and the woman decided to beat the man seriously. When the man saw that the fight was too hot for him, he ran out of the house, with the intention to report to the pastor and call him to settle the quarrel. But a few metres to the pastor's house, he discovered that, the pastor and his wife were also boxing each other. He stood and said, "Ah! I better go and sort out my own problem. If you are like that man, encourage yourself. Stand against all forms of anxiety. One great problem that God has with us is that, we hold on to our problems but we are not experts at solving them. At times when we have messed everything up, we carry the leftover to God.

3. **Believe that all things are possible**: Jesus said that, all things are possible to him that believes. Perhaps you have problems that seem to defy solution; you have come to your wits end. You have decided, "Well, this place is my last stop. I am going to run away from God." No, all things are possible to him that believes.

The Bible does not say that all things are possible to him that worries. When we say things are impossible, it means that we have arrived at self-defeat. God is a gentleman; He will not grab the problem out of your hand, if you do not hand it to Him. So, whatever the situation may be, believe that all things are possible. I remember the testimony of a six-year old boy who could neither walk nor talk. His mother carried him all over the place and at a point brought him to our crusade.

As the crusade was about to close, I said, "We have a project to do here and people should give to the Lord."

41

The woman cried and said, "I have been here for one week and nothing has happened; she took all the money she had and dumped it in the offering bag. It was then the word of knowledge came that, the boy had been healed .Right before her eyes, the first thing that happened was that, the bent bone of the boy stretched out and a cracking sound could be heard as it moved. By the time God finished with the boy, a medical doctor at the meeting could count 26 miracles performed on him. The enemy had finished his case completely, but God turned it around. That God is still around. So, see that possibility and you will see what the Lord will do.

4. **Do not give up**: When your eyes are turning red, do not give up. When life is becoming disjointed and disorganized, don't give up. When you feel you cannot take another step ahead, don't give up. When trials surround you everyday and your enemies are showing themselves as friends, don't give up. When you think that all is lost, don't give up. When all things are moving up and the road is so rough and tiring; you try to smile and the smile is hard-work or when the debts are so much, do not give up.

    Many strugglers have given up at the edge of success.
    One sister was praying, "O Lord, give me breakthrough."
    The Lord said, "You already have it." Still after five years there was no breakthrough. You know that God is a God of suddenlies. One morning, God sent an angel to give the sister what she wanted. The angel came to church before the service and waited for her to arrive, but that morning the devil went to her, to give her a satanic lecture.

A certain pastor said that the devil is a great pastor. He knows the house of every member, he knows their names, he knows where they work and he knows everything about them. He is present at every table where they eat; he is present at all their family meetings. No pastor can do all these.

The devil came to the sister and said: "Look at you; at your old age, you are sweeping the floor of the church, for the mates of your children, cleaning benches. Since you have been going there, what have you brought out of that place? Stop wasting your time."

And for the first time in five years, she listened to that lecture and did not go to the service, that day the angel came for her. The angel waited in vain till the end of the service. Well, the Bible says, "The word which I have spoken from my mouth shall not come back to me void." So, after the grace was said, the angel gave the blessing to somebody else and departed.

Many strugglers give up at the edge of success, but David encouraged himself in the Lord and his spirit became calm. While he was crying he could not hear God, but immediately he stopped crying and encouraged himself in the Lord, his spirit became calm. All the crying exercises did not let him hear God, but immediately he stopped crying and encouraged himself in the Lord, the voice of God came to him saying, "Surely you shall pursue, overtake and by all means recover."

Discouragement is a very clever spirit. If somebody used to run to service and now he is walking slowly to the place, the spirit of discouragement has started working. When someone who used to pray and smile, is now depressed and unhappy, the spirit is setting in. Discouragement has many powerful children, like fear, worry, depression, death, sickness and hindrances. That is why the Bible says, "Let not your heart be troubled." Get to the level where the devil will say, "This one? I am not able to defeat him."

The Bible says Paul and Silas prayed and sang praises to God in the prison. With all the wounds in their bodies, they just refused to be discouraged.

PRAYER POINTS

1. Every spirit of discouragement, I am not your candidate; I bind you, in the name of Jesus.
2. Every good thing I have lost because of discouragement, I recover it, in Jesus' name.
3. Every enemy of joy in my heart, fall down and die, in Jesus' name.
4. I pursue my enemies, I overtake them and I recover my stolen properties, in the name of Jesus.
5. I bind every spirit of evil expectation, in the name of Jesus.

CHAPTER SIX

KEEPING
THE FIRE

You cannot afford to be weak in this present generation, considering what is going on now and the wicked activities of the devil. You cannot afford to remain at the level of average power content. Immediately you are a threat to the devil, then you are qualified to be attacked. The moment the enemy sees your marriage as a danger and threat to his kingdom and you refuse to rise up against him, then there will be trouble.

Some years ago in South Africa, the witches gathered together and fasted 201 days against Christian marriages. Many of the Christian leaders were aware of the witchcraft prayer meeting; they just took it with levity and counted it as part of the normal works of the devil. But within a month the evil prayer meeting was held, marriages of Christians began to crash, until some intercessors gathered themselves to counter the devil's meeting. It was then that there was respite.

Lay your hands on your chest in desperation like a wounded lion and pray this prayer:

"Thou satanic prayer against the power of God in my life, die, in the name of Jesus."

TRUE LIFE CONFRONTATION

I have a friend, whom I can refer to as my father in the Lord; he is very much older than me. He shared something with me.

He said he went to visit one of his pastors, at a particular place. As he got to the place in his car, he expected to see members of the church, including his pastor, to come and welcome him. But to his greatest surprise, he could not see any of them around. What he saw was that, the front of the

46

church was filled with witch doctors, fetish priests, lodge members in their regalia and other people with terrible satanic weapons in their hands. Some of the people put on masquerade attires.

These satanic entities came to the old pastor and said, "Sir, we have been waiting for your arrival. Are you the General Overseer?" He said, "Yes, by the grace of God, I am the founder of this church." They said, "Are you the one that brought the present pastor here, to pastor this church?" The old pastor said, "Yes." These satanic men then said, "Take your dog away from this place, because since you brought him here, he has been a trouble maker in this place."

The old pastor asked, "What is the actual problem?" They said, "Since you sent this man to this place, he has converted nearly all the young men, that used to carry masquerades, and nobody is carrying masquerades again." They continued: "Since he came here, all witchdoctors have died in poverty, because there are no longer customers for them. And to worsen the case, the man will wake up in the night and move round people's houses, pointing at them while speaking one strange language. And as he speaks that strange language, we will start feeling uncomfortable. Therefore, take him away from here."

This old pastor said he pinched himself; to be sure it was not a dream. He had a face to face confrontation with evil powers.

THE OLD FASHIONED GOSPEL

When your power content is high, you will not be running from your enemies, but they will be making a plea unto you. Anytime they see you, they will panic. But unfortunately, this is not so for many people.

47

What is spiritual power? It is the ability to overcome the negative power that is working contrary to you. What is spiritual power? It is the ability to control.

When I got born again and was baptised in the Holy Spirit, I faced tough prayer challenges. Anyone who had received the baptism of the Holy Ghost in those days, was encouraged to pray in tongues for at least two hours everyday.

I challenge you too; pray in tongues for at least, 30 minutes everyday. You will then marvel, at how God's power will be lavished on you. If you can decide to wake up at midnight everyday, between 12.am and 3.00 am to pray, for one month; before the end of that month, you will become an entirely new person.

THE BENEFITS

I discovered that when I was practicing, speaking in tongues in prayer, for about two hours every day, my lecturers were running helter skelter, to satisfy me. Whenever I wanted to buy food, the seller would sell more than my money's worth. If I entered into the bus, most of the time, one person or the other would pay my transport fare. These are the things that could happen to you, whenever your power content is high.

Many of us do not know that we miss a lot of things, by living powerless lives. Many are yet to fully know that "ice cream Christianity" and "kindergarten prayer", cannot take us anywhere in God. Many are yet to understand, that there is no gentle method of arresting evil. It is very unfortunate that because of our powerlessness, the judge is becoming an accused; the person who is supposed to issue words of authority, is now being arrested.

THE PERIL OF POWERLESSNESS

If the kind of power God has destined for His children is in constant use by them, they would become a terror to the kingdom of darkness. When they speak, their words will carry weight. But, unfortunately, our lack of power in this generation has become rampant. We have concentrated our efforts on attachments, make-ups and wearing clothes that expose our nakedness. We concentrate our efforts on the wrong places; that is exactly what the enemy wants. Because we focus our attention in a wrong direction, several evil things are springing forth in our midst.

Sisters, who are supposed to be prophetesses of the Lord, cannot even hear from God. There are some, whom God wants to be discussing with, but He has refused talking to them, because of the idol of jewellery they are worshipping. Men are coming to God's house, but they lack God's power. The reason for lack of power is that, we are wrongly focused. If you are powerless, then you may be mince meat, in the mouth of the powers of darkness.

SHEEP DISGRACE

If you do not want to be wasted, you must concentrate on the power content of your inner man. It is an insult, for witchcraft, magicians and satanic agents to manipulate you. It is an assault to God, that you can be arrested through incantations and enchantments.

A woman came for prayers many years ago, she was a celebrity. Somebody entered into her shop and demanded to know how much she had sold. She told him, the person demanded the money and she gave him. The person again asked for the most expensive thing, she had in the shop, she told him and he said, she should bring it too, and she did. The person told the madam further, "I love this attire, how much did you buy it?" She told him. After that the person said, "Madam, I will not like to disgrace you, but you can just take the wrapper, while you give me the blouse." The woman agreed and gave him her blouse. Then, he said, "Bye-bye," and walked away.

When her eyes cleared, she started screaming and was reading Psalm 23. But how come the shepherd ran away, when a dubious person met her in the shop? I said, "Madam, do you want to change your focus?" She said, "Yes." I told her that, the most important thing is how powerful the inner man is. No matter how much the flesh is polished, one day, somebody will say, "Ashes for ashes, dust for dust," and that is all.

Are you there, buying special creams for your body, while the enemy is still pursuing you in the dream? You must retrace your steps.

It is compulsory for us to have adequate power, deposited in the inner man. We ought to be going from strength to strength, not from strength to weakness. What is needed these days is power from above, as opposed to powerlessness.

POWER ENCOUNTER

Oh that God will bless this country with just five Elijah's. If there are five Elijah's in this country, there would be perfect peace in the nation.

When power faces power, then the weaker power will pack up. When power faces power, one power will always supersede. One power must give way for the other.

If you take a cursory look at Acts 19, you will discover that the people of Ephesus were keenly interested in witchcraft. They were very much like the people of Nigeria today. Young men are using demonic powder to attract ladies to them. Some people will bury something in the cemetery for seven days, after which they will take the thing back and put it in their pocket for demonic activities. People kidnap others and use them to make charms, because they want money. Some take their bath with human blood every day. There are people who walk to market places, where there is a crowd to test juju on people. All kinds of evil things are happening.

There are satanic agents parading all over the place. These were the occurrences in the biblical Ephesus until the power of God arrested the situation.

PRAYER POINTS

I. Holy Ghost fire, fill my spirit, soul and body, in the name of Jesus.I. Every evil power influencing my life negatively, fall down and die, in the name of Jesus.

II. O Lord, visit my life with Your fire, in the name of Jesus.

III. I disapprove every satanic legal ground in my life, in the name of Jesus.

IV. Fire of God, consume every strange satanic material in my head, in the name of Jesus.

V. Every power that has vowed to make my life a

51

desert, fall down and die, in the name of Jesus.

VI.   Let stubborn problems in my life be disgraced, in the name of Jesus.

VII.   Every evil strongman walking along with me in the journey of my life, fall down and die, in the name of Jesus.

VIII.   Every evil covenant affecting my life, break by the power in the blood of Jesus.

IX.   Any curse operating on my life, preventing my moving forward, break, in the name of Jesus.

X.   Evil pronouncements against my life before any idol, die, in the name of Jesus.

XI.   Evil strongman holding on to any department of my life, loose your hold and die, in the name of Jesus.

XII.   Every root of the spirit of anger in my life, die, in the name of Jesus.

XIII.   Every satanic chain in my hands and legs, be cut off, in the name of Jesus.
Weariness in prayer, depart from my life, in the name of Jesus.

OTHER BOOKS BY DR. D. K. OLUKOYA

1. 20 Marching Orders To Fulfill Your Destiny
2. 30 Things The Anointing Can Do For You
3. A-Z of Complete Deliverance
4. Abraham's Children in Bondage
5. Be Prepared
6. Bewitchment must die
7. Biblical Principles of Dream Interpretation
8. Born Great, But Tied Down
9. Breaking Bad Habits
10. Breakthrough Prayers For Business Professionals
11. Brokenness
12. Bringing Down The Power of God
13. Can God?
14. Can God Trust You?
15. Command The Morning
16. Consecration Commitment & Loyalty
17. Contending For The Kingdom
18. Connecting to The God of Breakthroughs
19. Criminals In The House Of God
20. Dancers At The Gate of Death
21. Dealing With Hidden Curses
22. Dealing With Local Satanic Technology
23. Dealing With Satanic Exchange
24. Dealing With The Evil Powers Of Your Father's House
25. Dealing With Tropical Demons
26. Dealing With Unprofitable Roots
27. Dealing With Witchcraft Barbers
28. Deliverance By Fire
29. Deliverance From Spirit Husband And Spirit Wife
30. Deliverance From The Limiting Powers

YORUBA PUBLICATIONS

1.	ADURA AGBAYORI
2.	ADURA TI NSI OKE NIDI
3.	OJO ADURA

FRENCH PUBLICATIONS

1.	PLUIE DE PRIERE
2.	ESPIRIT DE VAGABONDAGE
3.	EN FINIR AVEC LES FORCES MALEFIQUES DE LA MAISON DE TON PERE
4.	QUE I'ENVOUTEMENT PERISSE
5.	FRAPPEZ I'ADVERSAIRE ET IL FUIRA
6.	COMMENT RECEVIOR LA DELIVRANCE DU MARI ET FEMME DE NUIT
7.	CPMMENT SE DELIVRER SOI-MEME
8.	POVOIR CONTRE LES TERRORITES SPIRITUEL
9.	PRIERE DE PERCEES POUR LES HOMMES D'AFFAIRES
10.	PRIER JUSQU'A REMPORTER LA VICTOIRE
11.	PRIERES VIOLENTES POUR HUMILIER LES PROBLEMES OPINIATRES
12.	PRIERE POUR DETRUIRE LES MALADIES ET INFIRMITES
13.	LE COMBAT SPIRITUEL ET LE FOYER
14.	BILAN SPIRITUEL PERSONNEL

ANNUAL 70 DAYS PRAYER AND FASTING PUBLICATIONS

1. Prayers That Bring Miracles
2. Let God Answer By Fire
3. Prayers To Mount With Wings As Eagles
4. Prayers That Bring Explosive Increase
5. Prayers For Open Heavens
6. Prayers To Make You Fulfil Your Divine Destiny
7. Prayers That Make God To Answer And Fight By Fire
8. Prayers That Bring Unchallengeable Victory And Breakthrough Rainfall Bombardments
9. Prayers That Bring Dominion Prosperity And Uncommon Success
10. Prayers That Bring Power And Overflowing Progress
11. Prayers That Bring Laughter And Enlargement Breakthroughs
12. Prayers That Bring Uncommon Favour And Breakthroughs
13. Prayers That Bring Unprecedented Greatness & Unmatchable Increase
14. Prayers That Bring Awesome Testimonies And Turn Around Breakthroughs

www.ingramcontent.com/pod-product-compliance
Lightning Source LLC
Chambersburg PA
CBHW062034040426
42447CB00010B/2280